BABY'S BREATH

BABY'S BREATH

Some RHYME and REASON

Spring 2015

To Mary Ellen,
My friend - Thank
you for the years of "TLC"
towards me. Please Enjoy
my musings on family, faith
And fun! You are the best!

STEVIE RAWLINGS

Stevie Rawlings

authorHOUSE®

AuthorHouse™ LLC
1663 Liberty Drive
Bloomington, IN 47403
www.authorhouse.com
Phone: 1-800-839-8640

Published by AuthorHouse   04/09/2014

ISBN: 978-1-4918-4186-0 (sc)
ISBN: 978-1-4918-4185-3 (e)

Library of Congress Control Number: 2013922433

TABLE OF CONTENTS

OVER ON YOUNG

(4917 Young Avenue, Indianapolis, Indiana)

Over on Young, Over on Young,

When life was an easy rhyme,

Sure, it was a street,

Yep, it was a house,

But mostly, it was a time.

When trees were lookouts, towels were capes,

And tents were made of sheets,

Dry logs, wet pups, and pipe tobacco

Never smelled as sweet—

Over on Young

When Mama's laps were softer,

Daddy's knees were stronger,

When bedtime rhymes were longer,

Over on Young

When Santa brought the tallest tree,

New dollies, trains and cap guns,

When every child was number 1—

Over on Young

From the hearth to the highest beam

Hymns in harmony were sung,

Didn't know what we'd become,

Over on Young

Over on Young, Over on Young,

When life was an easy rhyme.

Sure, it was a street,

Yep, it was a house,

But mostly, it was a time.

LULLABY

Daddy sleeps as the clock strikes three,

Baby talks to a raisin box,

Mama curls up on the couch for now,

And the rain sings softly to us all,

to us all.

Tea cups rest by the rocking chair,

Toy frog sleeps by the raisin box,

Music books wait for another day,

And the rain sings softly to it all,

to it all.

Daddy sleeps as the clock strikes four,

Baby needs more than the raisin box,

Mama holds Baby in the rocking chair,

And the rain sings softly for us all,

for us all.

OCTOBER MORNING

I saw a little squirrel

Near a Ginko tree,

Storing oh so much for winter,

Oh, so much for winter!

I marveled at him,

His ambition,

And instinctive wisdom.

He and I had much in common,

Living as neighbors on Senator Place.

May I follow his example,

Lest my winter come.

I saw a little girl

Near a Ginko tree,

Storing oh so much for winter,

Oh, so much for winter!

GENERATIONS

Silence for only a little while,

Replaced by sounds from a little one.

Illusion will have form, feel, life;

So quickly a life.

Fears give way to wonder,

As does pain to its cause.

One day its cause will speak—

Will speak long after I am silent.

TO LITTLE ONE

Waiting for "little one",

Our mandarin, our peach,

All manner of lightness is "little you",

And yet, beyond our reach.

Your Mom and Daddy love you,

Even sight unseen.

The sweetness of fresh orange

Holds your nursery, "tangerine".

Many years before your "hue",

Doc Leman named my aura too.

We are alike, little "punkin seed",

We will share a dreamsicle or two.

I feel your smile beyond the miles,

So puckered and all knowing.

Come outside now,

Enjoy the space,

Where all can see you growing.

HEAR US, CYRUS

Hear us, Cyrus, hear us!

We love it when you're near us.

That twinkle in your eye says,

You value what's between us.

Your "accents" will delight us.

Piano musings entertain us.

Your drawings will amuse us.

Your experiments may change us.

Hear us, Cyrus, hear us!

We love it when you're near us.

That wisdom in your heart says,

Someday you may lead us.

Your Algebra's the "cat's meow",

An Einstein for here and now.

You bring the world a drum-roll, Wow!

Hear us, Cyrus, hear us!

AUGUST, MIGHTY AUGUST

August, mighty August,

Born to be robust.

Accustomed to a race or two,

You'll leave most in your dust!

With writing, reading, storytelling,

Your lust for these a must.

Those talents shine, with "might for right".

Your goodness you can trust!

August, mighty August,

Born to be robust.

Accustomed to a drill or two,

For you, a win is just!

Your chimpanzees and cityscapes

Are standouts we all treasure.

Your "pop"s and "pow"s and "choo", "ching" "p'chow",

Are sounds that bring you pleasure.

Deliveries of pies and cakes

Show kindness beyond measure.

Your sights, your sounds, your will we trust,

August, mighty August.

WIT AND WISDOM

Ingrid in my day,

Ingrid in my heart,

With Mama's brow and Daddy's smile,

A perfect Rockies work of art.

Ingrid in my arms,

So light, so warm, so new,

With thoughts and laughter you can start,

Colorado days are just for you.

LITTLE INGRID

Little Ingrid, little Ingrid,

Come on out to play.

Over mountains, over pastures, over forests,

Come our way.

Bring your laughter, bring your "Gatie",

Come and spend a holiday.

Little Ingrid, little Ingrid,

Come on out to play.

We'll have waffles and some berries,

And bananas every day.

You'll bring sunshine to New Jersey,

And we'd love for you to stay!

Little Ingrid, little Ingrid,

Come on out to play.

We're waiting for you—Get your coat,

Make Gramma and Pappaw's Day!

HAPPY ST. PATRICK'S DAY

for Cyrus and August

In the land of "BRIGHT YOUNG LADS",

There lived two brothers fine.

Many their dances and many their songs,

Young ladies, GET IN LINE.

A lilt was in their name,

They were destined sure for fame.

These TWO boys and "BRIGHT, YOUNG LADS"

Were ONE and the same.

They wore their green and smiled their smiles,

The happiest of time.

Their Gramma missed them so.

She wrote to celebrate in RHYME.

SCHOOL DAYS 1990

Ya hear . . .

"Wutcha", "Can ah", "Mrs. Lady"?

"Git-eem off mah back!"

"Bland monkey!", "Git-cho glasses"

("Brung 'em in a sack")

"Dat's Bad!" "Git da bongos",

"Hurry up wit dat!".

"Yes'm, yes'm, Mrs. Lady",

"Ah's too old fo dat".

"Boy yo Mutha!" "Yo Grandmutha!"

"Man, ah need a pass".

"Wutcha", "Can ah", "Mrs. Lady"?

"Dat seat hurts mah ass!"

LYRIC LAMENT

A Tribute to Myrna

The Premiere of "Lyric Lament" was performed by Myrna Reynolds on Sunday, March 11, 2012, in Berkman Recital Hall at the Hartt School of Music in West Harford, Connecticut. It was written as a tribute to my dear friend and kindred spirit in music and in life who found it difficult, (often) being a soprano, to memorize lyrics. "Lyric Lament" was a "tour de force" for Myrna, both vocally and comedically, with musical references intentionally written to pay tribute to her singing career. It was a "showstopper" amongst the more "traditional" solo, vocal music presented that afternoon, composed entirely by women. The musical setting of "Lyric Lament" was composed by Stacey Cahoon. Thank you, Stacey, for accessing Myrna's agility from classical obligato to blues in your score! Thank you, Myrna, for creating a soprano SHOW PIECE!

LYRIC LAMENT

(The first line of a BLUES song is always repeated)

WHY CAN'T A SOPRANO JUST SING

"VOH-DEE-OH-DOH"?

WHY CAN'T A SOPRANO JUST SING

"VOH-DEE-OH—DOH"?

BASSIE AND BENNIE could JUST BLOW,

YOYO CAN JUST BOW,

WHY CAN'T A SOPRANO JUST SING

"VOH-DEE-OH-DOH"?

Scat's where it's at,

Where words are old hat,

SIMPLICITY'S for those in the know.

NO more ANGST or hours drilling—

GERMAN, FRENCH OR L'ITALIANOOOOOHHH

How nice to only memorize the "Scoobie-do-bee-WAH"

or "Doo-be-doo-be-OH" . . . .

OOOOOHHH, but NO, no, no—

WHY CAN'T A SOPRANO JUST SING

"VOH-DEE-OH-DOH"?

WHY CAN'T A SOPRANO JUST SING

"VOH-DEE-OH—DOH"?

BASSIE AND BENNIE could JUST BLOW,

YOYO CAN JUST BOW,

WHY CAN'T A SOPRANO JUST SING

"VOH-DEE-OH-DOH"?

If VAUGHN MONROE, Tormé, Dean and Ella

Could leave the words and GO,

No one needs 'em, no one READS 'em!

Forget the words! Get on with the show!—

AND SO,—

WHY—OHHHH

WHY CAN'T A SOPRANO JUST SING

"VOH-DEE-OH-DOH"?

WHY CAN'T A SOPRANO JUST SING

"VOH-DEE-OH-DOH"?

BASSIE AND BENNIE could JUST BLOW,

YOYO CAN JUST BOW,

WHY CAN'T A SOPRANO JUST SING

"VOH-DEE-OH-DOH"?

Mozart got it right with his Queen of the Night,

("Ah, ah, ah, ah, ah, ah-ah-ah"! "Ah-

ah-ah-ah-ah ah-ah-ah"!)

He left the words for Sarostro!! Bravo!!! Oh—

—Tom Jones knows how to kill us with

his "Whoa-oh, Whoa, Whao-oh"!

—Bing can get away with "Boo-Boo-Boo-Boo"!

—The Caribbean rocks with Belafonte's

Day-oh, day-ay-ay-ay-oh"!

—Even Santa keeps it simple with his "Ho, Ho, Ho"!!

Please forgive this sad soprano who sings

"<u>VO</u>-<u>VO</u>-<u>VO</u>-DEE-OH-DOH"!!!

WHY CAN'T A SOPRANO JUST SING

"VOH-DEE-OH-DOH"?

WHY CAN'T A SOPRANO JUST SING

"VOH-DEE-OH—DOH"?

BASSIE AND BENNIE could JUST BLOW,

YOYO CAN JUST BOW,

WHY CAN'T A SOPRANO JUST SING

"VOH-DEE-OH-DOH"?

Please, please forgive this sad soprano who

sings "<u>VO</u>-<u>VO</u>-<u>VO</u>-DEE-OH-DOH"!!!

IN GRATITUDE

Poetry is accessible.

Writing poetry is possible.

Poetry is sharing.

My Daddy taught me these truths—perhaps accidentally.
I had the good fortune to hear some of his words ring in
my ears—over the years. The following poem is one of
his best.

THE LEAST ONE

By John Henry Reider

To Marcy

The older ones have all passed out

And the dogs are comfy too.

Mama's out with the girls tonight,

But sleep I cannot do.

The least one's still a-talkin'

Tho it's gettin' mighty late.

And now she'll try a song or two

To stall the Sandman's date.

Course I'll be up and gone at dawn

And I won't get home til night,

But I don't see much of the little ones,

And soft singin' is alright.

The older kids grew by so fast

And us tryin' to get a start,

I hardly knew my name was "Dad"

And I 'bout forgot the word "sweetheart."

But now I've got this one last chance,

To really know a little kid.

They say they all looked just like her

And I'm sure hopin' that they did.

Cause I just couldn't stand to think

That I missed so many times

When she pats me like I was a pup

And when she says her little rhymes.

So if she chatters for a while,

And I miss an hour or so of sleep,

It's cause Daddy treasures Love and Life

And thinks Rest and Things are pretty cheap.

TO DADDY

A rainy Sunday afternoon comes.

A Schönburg folksong rings
With "Poppy" helping at the cadences.

Is "Rosy" helping with *Wild Colonial Boy?*

Is the smell of frying chicken drifting by you too?

Scent, Sight, and Sound are a daughter's gifts.

THE FATE OF LEAVES

I've seen leaves running from my feet.

I've seen leaves rolling in the sun.

Their acrobatics in the trees,

Autumnal games 'til winter comes.

They quilt the hills with colored puffs,

To warm the land of man.

But when they're quilted by the snow,

I question Nature's plan.

THANK YOU TO STEPHEN AND OWEN—

The "Boohoo Bouquet" received its "world premiere" at the Grand 1894 Opera House in Galveston, Texas, on Sunday, July 21, 2013. Inspired by the talent, dedication and vision of <u>Stephen Roddy</u>, the mere poetic "buds" that I shared with him became a staged, musical reality! The Houston Children's Chorus, under his baton, brought the poems to life with their innocent vocal clarity and thoughtful attention to detail. Deepest gratitude is extended to <u>Owen Robbins</u> for the stylistically varied musical score; each a perfect match for the poems' intent. I am so grateful to these kind, talented friends!

THE BOOHOO BOUQUET

A Garland of Neglected Flerrrs

FORSYTHIA

Forsythia, Forsythia,

I'd like to have a sniff-a-ya.

I've never had a whiff-a-ya,

But maybe in the Spring.

The bees'll get a nip-a-ya,

Dee-do-dah'll get a zip-a-ya,

My right hand has a grip-a-ya,

A bouquet in the Spring.

Oh, dear. I took a sniff-a-ya.

Oh, no! There ain't no whiff-a-ya,

No honeysuckle drip-a-ya,

But you still make me sing.

Forsythia, Forsythia,

It's a bloomin' bliss-a-ya.

I'm blowin' you a kiss,

Cause you're plum perty in the Spring.

HYACINTH

Hyacinth, oh, Hyacinth,

Peekin' through the picket fence,

With pink and purple so intense,

Where is your poetry?

There's verse a-plenty from the gents,

'Bout roses, lilies, or violets,

The Emersons and Tennysons,

Missed seein' your rare beauty.

This over-sight makes no sense.

May I put in my two cents?

Your fragrance rates a document,

Your name, a melody.

Hyacinth, oh, Hyacinth,

Peekin' through the picket fence,

Hang on to your confidence,

Your poem's safe with me.

CLOVER

for my Brother

Clover, sweet Clover,

In pastures all over,

Both red and white puffs,

The ponies find you.

Clover, sweet Clover,

In school yards all over,

So soft in the sunshine,

Outfielders love you.

Your racing lanes of clover chains,

And "crowns" that little winners claim,

Imagining the summer games,

All soundly thanks to you.

Clover, sweet Clover,

The Shamrocks best cover,

There's lilt in your meadows,

The Irish wear you.

Clover, sweet Clover,

The battle is over,

The mowers can't beat you,

You're growin' for you.

HOLLYHOCKS

for my Mother

Hollyhocks see roller skates,
Hollyhocks hear "Kick the can!"
Assigned to alleys, barns or gates,
Around since fun began.

"Whirring" wheels and "moo"s and "howdy"s
Pass the sunkissed Hollyhocks.
Blossoms bend toward liquid laughter
From hopscotch and rollin' rocks.

See'n Mornin' Glory, Rose of Sharon,
Or Flowers of the Sun,
A childish eye investigates,
A-pickin' Hollyhocks, bar none.

Hollyhocks ride roller skates,
Hollyhocks crown dolly's hair.
Down the alley, through the gate,
And never pay a fare.

DANDELIONS

for Morgan

Dandelions rule, dandelions roar,

Bravely change their habitat to

Where they weren't before.

Dandelions dare to grow,

Far from early roots.

Movin's easy! Fly and blow!

You and WIND are in cahoots.

Wild and widespread

On your way,

With this parting wish—

Before your mane turns white as snow

Be someone's dinner dish.

Dandelions sing, dandelions soar,

Smilin' in their habitat,

Where they weren't before.

SNAPDRAGONS

for Kevin

Snapdragons know to listen,

Although they're never weak.

Just pinch them in the middle,

And they'll be sure to speak.

This fire-breathing flower

Is no myth, but miracle.

So tall its blossom tower,

Loved by children, wives, and all.

No lightening might or crack of ice

Can bring Snapdragons down.

In blooms we see their destiny

Bolt boldly from the ground.

Snapdragons find the water's edge,

Their happy place to be.

If the metaphor were man,

We'd see him on one knee.

Snapdragons know the winter

Will be followed by the Spring.

Let's pinch them in the middle,

And they'll be sure to sing.

PATIENCE

Cleaning my Denver garnet

Staring at my Budapest blouse

I know you are making magic

With Magic Flute.

Sharing from a distance

Is what we know so well.

Close would be so nice,

But I keep close all that I can,

Because I trust that TIME is our friend.

TIME will see us close

And phone booths and packing

Will be a memory.

FOR AUNT MILLIE

Take me from my garden now,

I am at peace with Thee.

Planting's done and buds are full,

Lord, abide with me.

I kiss the earth,

I hear the song the angels sing to me.

Take me from my garden now,

I am at peace with Thee.

**Blank pages available for musings by
my children and grandchildren—**

40986489R00032

Made in the USA
Lexington, KY
25 April 2015